A Collection of Dynamic Programming Interview Questions Solved in C++

Antonio Gulli

ISBN: 1495320480
ISBN-13: 978-1495320484

Dynamic programming is the first of a series or 25 mini books devoted to algorithms, problem solving, and c++ programming

DEDICATION

To Lorenzo, my first child.

With the hope that you will enjoy mathematics for the rest of your life, as much as you enjoyed solving problem 8 when you were 10 years old

ACKNOWLEDGMENTS

Thanks to Gaetano Mendola for code reviewing

i

Table of Contents

Table of Contents 2

Dynamic programming: the art of solving simple problems first................5

1.   Fibonacci numbers 6

2.   Binomial Coefficient 7

3.   Max sub-array problem - given an array of integers, compute the largest sum continuous sub array 8

4.   Catalan Numbers..10

5.   Integer Knapsack – A knapsack has max capacity C and there are n items each with weight $w[i]$ and value $v[i]$. Maximize the value in the knapsack without exceeding its max capacity............................12

6.   Edit Distance -– Given two strings, compute the edit distance between them 13

7.   Neat Print – Given a sequence of words and a max number of words which can be put in a line, print the sequence of words neatly. Assume that no word is split across lines. 15

8.   Eggs Drop – Given k eggs and n floors in a building, find the minimum number of trials required to determine the lowest floor from which an egg can be dropped without getting broken....................17

9.   Jump Stairs – There is a stair with n steps. You can climb either one step or two steps at a time. How many different ways there are to climb the stair? 19

10.   Jumping Array – Given an array of non-negative numbers, start at the first element and reach the end with a minimum number of jumps. A jump cannot exceed the length contained in the current position............21

11.   Dice -– Given n dice, count how many ways to get sum s.............22

12.   Coin Change – Given n dollars, how many different ways there are to make the change into a set of coins S? 23

13.   Longest Palindrome String – Given a string, compute the longest palindromic substring...24

14.   String Palindromes -– Given a string, find the minimum number of characters to be inserted for converting the string into a palindrome 26

15.   LCS -– Given two strings *S1* and i, find the longest common substring 27

16.   LCS – Given two strings, find the longest common subsequence ..29

17.   LIS – Given an array of integers, find the longest increasing subsequence 31

18.   Bridge Matching – n cities are on the northern bank of a river and n cities are on the southern bank. You can build a bridge only between cities with the same number 32

19.   LBS – Given an array of integers, find the longest bitonic sequence 32

20.   Box Stacking – Given a set of *3d* boxes, compute the largest stack of boxes. A box can be stacked only on top of another box with larger base.   33

21.   Sum Subset -– Given an array of integers of size *n*, partition it in such a way that the two subsets have equal sum *s* 34

22.   Partition Set – partition a multiset S of positive integers into two subsets *S1* and *S2*, such that the sum of the numbers in *S1* equals the sum of the numbers in *S2* 36

23.   Segment Partition -– Given a segment of integer length *n,* cut it into different integer parts in such a way to maximize the product of the lengths of all parts. 37

24.   Cutting a Rod – given a rod of length *n* and a vector of prices for different lengths, cut the rod for maximizing the gain...............................38

25.   Bellman-Ford – Given a graph *G* and a source vertex, find the shortest paths from the source *src* to all vertices. The graph may contain negative edges 39

26.   Max Submatrix 0/1 - Given a matrix consisting only of 0s and 1s, find the maximum size square sub-matrix with all 1s 40

27.   Matrix Parenthesization -- Given a set of *m* Matrices find the most efficient way of multiplying them 41

28. Max Submatrix – Given a matrix of size *n x n* find the maximum sum rectangle 43

29. Given a Binary Search Tree, find the size of the largest independent set of nodes 44

30. Optimal Binary Tree – given a set *S* of tuples *<k, freq[k]>* , where *k* is an integer and *freq[k]* is the number of times that *k* has been observed, build a binary search three such that the total cost of all single searches is minimized 46

31. Boolean Parenthesization – given a Boolean expression of and, or, xor, true, false, find the number of ways to parenthesize and evaluate to true   48

32. Games of Coins – a set of coins are aligned and two players can pick one coin from each side in turn. Maximize the value of the coins picked by the first player 49

33. Maximum value contiguous subsequence – given an array of real numbers, find a contiguous subsequence with max sum *s* 50

34. Balanced partition – given an array of integers between 0 and *M*, divide the integers into two sets such that the difference of their sums is minimized 50

35. Scheduling – given n jobs, each one with a processing time ti a profit pi and a deadline di, maximize the profit 51

36. Stock prices – Given a histogram array of unsigned integers encoding the price of a stock title during the previous year, compute the area for the largest rectangle contained in this histogram 52

37. Ship Battle – Given a matrix *M* and an array *V*, match the array in the matrix 53

Appendix 56

Dynamic programming: the art of solving simple problems first

Dynamic programming (DP) solves intricate problems by breaking them down into simpler components. DP can be applied to problems exhibiting two properties: *overlapping subproblems* and *optimal substructure*.

Overlapping subproblems means that any recursive algorithm solving the problem should solve the same subproblems over and over, rather than generating new subproblems. Optimal substructure means that any optimal solution can be constructed efficiently from the optimal solutions of its subproblems. In other words, suppose that each subproblem has its own cost function: the optimal substructure implies that the minima of each of these cost functions can be found as the minima of the global cost function restricted to the same *subsets*.

DP pursues to solve each subproblem only once, as a result reducing the number of computations. After the solution to a given subproblem has been computed, it is stored in a table or "memoized". Next time the same solution is required, it is simply looked up. DP solves problems in either two methods:

a) Top-down approach: This is a consequence of the recursive mathematical definition associated to many DP problems.

b) Bottom-up approach: This requires a reformulation of the recursive mathematical definition where subproblems are solved first and their solutions used to build-on and achieve solutions for bigger subproblems

In this book we will review a collection of Dynamic programming problems, their solution, and the C++ code related to them. Many of those problems are commonly asked during interviews and can be frequently found on Internet web sites devoted to interviews' preparation.

5

1. Fibonacci numbers

Solution

The first two numbers in the Fibonacci sequence are 0 and 1, and each subsequent number is the sum of the previous two. By describing the numbers in his book *Liber Abaci*, Leonardo Fibonacci introduced the sequence to Western European mathematics in 1200, although the sequence had been described earlier in Indian mathematics.

Fibonacci numbers are mathematically defined as

$$f(n) = \begin{cases} f(n-1) + f(n-2) & n \geq 1 \\ 1 & n = 1 \\ 0 & n = 0 \end{cases}$$

Code

It is trivial to write a recursive solution directly derived from the mathematical formulation. Here we provide an implementation where Fibonacci is computed at compile time leveraging the power of templates.

```cpp
template <int N>
struct CTFibonacci {
  static constexpr int value() {
    return CTFibonacci<N-1>::value() +
           CTFibonacci<N-2>::value();
  }
};

template <>
struct CTFibonacci<1> {
  static constexpr int value() {
    return 1;
  }
};

template <>
struct CTFibonacci<0> {
  static constexpr int value() {
    return 0;
  }
};
```

Complexity

Complexity is here exponential since $T(n) = T(n-1) + T(n-2) + 1 \cong (\dfrac{1+\sqrt{5}}{2})^n \cong 2^n$. An alternative and more efficient solution memorizes the intermediate results and it avoids to recompute the same sub-problem for multiple times. A solution is:

Code

```cpp
unsigned int Fibonacci(unsigned int n)
{
  int a, b, sum;
  a = 0; b = 1; sum = a + b;
  if (n <= 1) return n;
  for (unsigned int i = 2; i < n; ++i)
  {
    a = b;
    b = sum;
    sum = a + b;
  }
  return sum;
}
```

Complexity

Linear in time and constant in space

2. Binomial Coefficient

The binomial coefficient indexed by n and k and denoted by $\binom{n}{k}$ is the coefficient of the x^k term in the polynomial expansion of the binomial power $(1 + x)^n$. The value of this coefficient is given by $\dfrac{n!}{k!(n-k)!}$.

Solution

Computing the binomial coefficient directly from the closed formula

$\binom{n}{k} = \dfrac{n!}{k!(n-k)!}$ would be inefficient. However, we can prove by induction that $\binom{n}{k} = \binom{n-1}{k-1} + \binom{n-1}{k}$ and we know that $\binom{n}{0} = 1$ and $\binom{0}{k} = 0$.

Therefore, we have a direct way to compute the binomial coefficient with dynamic programming. Note that Matrix is a class defined in the appendix.

Code

```cpp
unsigned int bin(unsigned int n, unsigned int k,
                 Matrix<int> & table)
{
  std::cout << "n=" << n << " k=" << k << std::endl;
  if (n == 0) return 0;

  if (!table(n - 1, k - 1))
    table(n - 1, k - 1) = bin(n - 1, k - 1, table);
  if (!table(n - 1, k))
    table(n - 1, k) = bin(n - 1, k, table);

  return table(n - 1, k - 1) + table(n - 1, k);
}

unsigned int binomial(unsigned int n, unsigned int k)
{
  if (k == 0) return 1;
  if (n == 0) return 0;

  Matrix<int> table(n + 1, k + 1, 0);
  for (unsigned int i = 0; i <= n; i++)
    table(i , 0) = 1;

  return bin(n, k, table);
}
```

Complexity

Linear in time $O(n)$. Space occupancy is $O(n\,k)$

3. Max sub-array problem - given an array of integers, compute the largest sum continuous sub array

Solution

This problem is a little gem. An elegant solution has been provided by Kadane.[1] The key intuition for this algorithm is illustrated by this picture

max_so_far represents the maximum value computed before analysing the current subsequence, while $max\_endiding\_here$ represents the maximum for the current subsequence. If $max\_(endiding\_here) \leq 0$, we violate the sequence continuity and therefore we can safely reset $max\_(endiding\_here) = 0$, a value which represents the empty string. If $max\_endiding\_here \leq max\_so\_far$, then we have found a new maximum and we can update the max_so_far accordingly:

Code

```cpp
int maxSubArraySum(const std::vector<int> & v)
{
  int max_so_far = 0, max_ending_here = 0;
  for (unsigned int i = 0; i < v.size(); ++i)
  {
    max_ending_here = max_ending_here + v[i];
    if (max_ending_here < 0)
      max_ending_here = 0;
    if (max_so_far < max_ending_here)
      max_so_far = max_ending_here;
  }
  return max_so_far;
}
```

The second implementation also returns the start and the end point for the max continuous sequence:

```cpp
int kadane(const std::vector<int> & v,
           int & start, int & finish)
{
  int maxSum = -std::numeric_limits<int>::max(), sum = 0;
  unsigned int left = 0, right = 0;
  start = finish = 0;
```

---

[1] http://en.wikipedia.org/wiki/Kadane%27s_algorithm

```
    for (unsigned int i = 0; i < v.size(); ++i) {
      sum += v[i];
      if (sum > maxSum) {
        maxSum = sum;
        finish = right = i;
        start  = left;
      } else if (sum < 0) {
        sum = 0;
        left = right = i+1;
      }
    }
    return maxSum;
  }
```

Complexity

Linear in the size of the input $O(n)$

4. Catalan Numbers

Catalan numbers are mathematically defined as:

$$C(n+1) = \begin{cases} 1 & n = 0 \\ \sum_{i=0}^{n} C(i)C(n-i) & n > 0 \end{cases}$$

Those numbers have multiple applications in combinatorics. For example: $C(n)$ counts the number of expressions containing n pairs of parentheses which are correctly matched (e.g. $C(3) = 5$ represents ((())) ()(()) ()()() (())() (()())). Also, $C(n)$ is the number of different ways $n + 1$ factors can be completely parenthesized (e.g. $C(3) = 5$ represents ((ab)c)d (a(bc))d (ab)(cd) a((bc)d) a(b(cd))). In addition, $C(n)$ is also the number of full binary trees with $n + 1$ leaves. For a complete description of the applications please refer Wikipedia[2].

Solution

The solution provided is directly implementing the recursive definition.

---

[2] http://en.wikipedia.org/wiki/Catalan_number

Code

```cpp
unsigned int cat(unsigned int n,
                 std::vector<unsigned int> & table)
{
  if (n == 0) return 1;

  for (unsigned int i = 0; i < n; i++)
  {
    if (!table[i])
      table[i] = cat(i, table);
    if (!table[n - 1 - i])
      table[n - 1 - i] = cat(n - 1 - i, table);

    table[n] += table[i] * table[n - 1 - i];
  }
  return table[n];
}
```

Complexity

Linear in the size of the input, $O(n)$

Solution

Notice that we can leverage the symmetry in the definition. For instance
$C4 = C0 * C3 + C1 * C2 + C2 * C1 + C3 * C0 = 2 * (C0 * C3 + C1 * C2)$.

This observation leads to the following recursive implementation.

Code

```cpp
unsigned int catalan2(unsigned int n)
{
  if (n == 0) return 1;
  unsigned int sum = 0;
  for (unsigned int i = 0; i < n/2; ++i) {
    sum += catalan(i)*catalan(n-1-i);
  }
  sum *= 2;
  if (n % 2) {
    unsigned int c = catalan(n/2);
    sum += c*c;
  }
  return sum;
```

        }

5. Integer Knapsack – A knapsack has max capacity C and there are n items each with weight $w[i]$ and value $v[i]$. Maximize the value in the knapsack without exceeding its max capacity

Solution

An item can be inserted in the knapsack or not: if the nth item is inserted, then the total value contained in the knapsack will increase of $v[n]$ and the capacity C will decreases of $w[n]$. If the item is not inserted, than the capacity will remain unchanged. This means that the solution can be then obtained recursively. Mathematically, we can define:

$$k(C, n) =$$

$$\begin{cases} 0 & n = 0 \,||\, C = 0 \\ k(C, n-1) & w[n] > C \\ max(k(C, n-1), v[n] + k(C - w[n], n-1)) & o.w. \end{cases}$$

In the remaining, we provide two different solutions: the first is top-down and recursive, while the second is based on dynamic programming and it is built bottom-up by storing partial results in a support array mem.

Code

```cpp
unsigned int knapRecursive(const unsigned int C,
                           const unsigned int w[],
                           const unsigned int v[],
                           const unsigned int n)
{
  if (n == 0 || C == 0)
    return 0;

  if (w[n - 1] > C)
    return knapRecursive(C, w, v, n - 1);

  else return std::max(v[n - 1] +
            knapRecursive(C - w[n - 1], w, v, n - 1),
            knapRecursive(C, w, v, n - 1));
```

```
}

unsigned int knapSack(const unsigned int C,
                      const unsigned int w[],
                      const unsigned int v[],
                      const unsigned int n)
{
  Matrix<unsigned int> table(n + 1, C + 1);

  for (unsigned int i = 0; i <= n; ++i)
    for (unsigned int j = 0; j <= C; ++j)
    {
      if (i == 0 || j == 0)
        table(i, j) = 0;
      else if (w[i - 1] <= j)
        table(i, j) =
          std::max(v[i - 1]  + table(i - 1, j - w[i - 1]),
                   table(i - 1, j));
      else
        table(i, j) = table(i - 1, j);
    }
  return table(n, C);
}
```

Complexity

Pseudolinear in time $O(n\,C)$ and Pseudolinear in space $O(n\,C)$

6. Edit Distance –– Given two strings, compute the edit distance between them

Solution

The edit distance is the minimum number of edits required to convert one string into another. For simplicity, we assume that the cost of insertion and deletion is 1. Consider two strings $S1[1, ...m]$ and $S2[1, ...n]$, we can define a cursor $0 \leq i < m$ for scanning S1 and a cursor $0 \leq j < n$ for scanning S2. The edit distance $E(i,j)$ is defined as it follows:

$$E(i,j) = \begin{cases} E(i-1, j-1) & \text{if } S1[i] == S2[j] \\ min(E(i-1, j-1), E(i, j-1), E(i-1, j)+1 & \text{o.w.} \end{cases}$$

In other words: if the characters are aligned, the edit distance for the problem $E(i,j)$ will not increase, otherwise we need to align the strings by reducing the size of S1, or S2 or both.

Now let's consider the base cases. Clearly, $E(0,0) = 0$ because this case represents the empty strings. We can also define $E(i,0) = i$ and $(0,j) = j$, because in this case we are comparing a string of length i (respectively j) with the empty string. We can use the above definition for computing the edit distance by tabulating all the values $1 \leq i \leq n, \ 1 \leq j \leq m$ with complexity $O(n\,m)$.

However, we can significantly improve the complexity by taking into account that we only need the input from the previous column in the table for computing the current column. This will allow us to require only $O(max(n, m))$. The code uses initialize the column $prevCol[j] = i$ for each $0 \leq j \leq n$ and this represents the maximum cost for position j. Then, we have two loops. The most external loop scans the string $S1$ for each $0 \leq i < m$ and it initializes $col[0] = i + 1$ which the maximum cost for the position. The internal loop scans the string $S2$ for each $0 \leq j < n$ and updates the edit distance value by directly applying the recursive definition. When the internal loop is concluded the columns col and $prevCol$ are swapped and the scan of $S1$ continues.

There are situations where it is appropriate to have different costs according to the specific edit operations (delete, insert) required to align the strings. Those changes are left as an exercise for the reader.

Code

```
unsigned int editDistance(const std::string &s1,
                          const std::string & s2)
{
    const size_t len1 = s1.size(), len2 = s2.size();
    std::vector<unsigned int> col(len2 + 1),
                prevCol(len2 + 1);

    std::iota(prevCol.begin(), prevCol.end(), 0);

    for (unsigned int i = 0; i < len1; ++i) {
        col[0] = i + 1;
```

```
        for (unsigned int j = 0; j < len2; ++j)
            col[j + 1] = std::min(1 + col[j],
                std::min(1 + prevCol[j],
                    prevCol[j] +
                        (s1[i] == s2[j] ? 0 : 1)));
        col.swap(prevCol);
    }
    return prevCol[len2];
}
```

Complexity

Complexity is $O(max(n, m))$

7. Neat Print – Given a sequence of words and a max number of words which can be put in a line, print the sequence of words neatly. Assume that no word is split across lines.

Solution

Let $len[i]$ be the length of word w_i. Intuitively, the cost of the first word is $c[0] = max - len[0]$ and for the remaining words we can initially define $c[i] = max - len[i]$. Also, let $M[i] = \infty$, $0 \leq i < n$ and consider the following recurrence, where we build the optimal cost for word i, by considering the optimal cost for word $i - 1$:

$$M[i] = \begin{cases} c[i] & i = 0 \\ M[i - 1] + c[i] & 0 < i < n \end{cases}$$

However this definition is not yet meeting our goal for two reasons.

First, $c[i]$ only considers the cost of the previous word, while it should consider all the words that can fit a line up to a maximal cost max. Therefore we need to redefine $c[i]$ in such a way to accumulate the cost of the previous words and stop before at the point where this cost becomes negative. Intuitively for each given word we need to scan no more than a max position backwards. This can be addressed by defining

$$c[i] = max - len[i] - \sum_{j=f}^{i-1} len[j] + 1$$

for a leftmost word $0 \le f < i$ such that $c[i] \ge 0$.

Second, the cost should be non-linear because we want to balance across lines (e.g. leaving two positions in one same line should intuitively cost more than leaving a position in one and the other position in another line). This requirement can be fulfilled in multiple ways, for instance by

defining $$c[i] = (max - len[i] - \sum_{j=f}^{i-1} len[j] + 1)^2$$ or more conveniently for

bitwise computation: $c[i] = 2^{(max - len[i] - \sum_{j=f}^{i-1} len[j] + 1)}$.

To summarize our goal is to find:

$\min f : 0 \le f < i$ such that $(max - len[i] - \sum_{j=f}^{i-1} len[j] + 1 > 0)$. In the code the vector M will contain final decreasing values containing the residuals for each word added to a given line. The values will increase again anytime that there is a need to change line.

Code

```
void neatPrint(std::vector<unsigned int> & M,
            const std::vector<unsigned int> & length,
            unsigned int max, int n)
{
    int penalty;
    for (int i = 0; i < n; i++)
    {
        penalty = max - length[i];
        M[i] = std::min(M[i], (i - 1 < 0 ? 0 : M[i - 1]) +
            (1 << penalty));
        for (int j = i - 1; j >= 0; j--)
        {
            penalty -= (length[j] + 1);
            if (penalty < 0)
                break;  // generate next line
```

```
        M[i] = std::min(M[i],
            ((j - 1 < 0) ? 0 : M[j - 1]) +
            (1 << penalty));
      }
    }
}

void solveNeatPrint(const std::vector<unsigned int> &
length, unsigned int max)
{
    int n = length.size();
    std::vector<unsigned int> M(n,
        std::numeric_limits<unsigned int>::max());
    neatPrint(M, length, max, n);
    for (int i = 0; i < n; ++i)
        std::cout << M[i] << ' ';
    std::cout << std::endl;
}
```

Complexity

Note that $M[i]$ can be computed in linear time of the input size, while $c[i]$ can be computed in $O(max)$ time.

8. Eggs Drop – Given k eggs and n floors in a building, find the minimum number of trials required to determine the lowest floor from which an egg can be dropped without getting broken.

Solution

This is a classical puzzle, frequently asked during interviews. Let $eggDrops(k, n)$ be the minimum number of attempts given k eggs and n floors. A dynamic solution can be computed by considering that when we drop an egg from floor f there are only two possible outcomes:

   a) If the egg breaks, then we have $k - 1$ eggs and we need to check the $f - 1$ floor

   b) If the egg does not break, then we have k eggs and the remaining $n - f$ floors left

Since we want to minimize the number of attempts, in the worst scenario we have to consider the maximum between a) and b). The relation then becomes:

$$eggDrops(k, n) =$$

$$1 + min_{1 \leq f \leq n}[max(eggDrops(k - 1, f - 1), eggDrops(k, n - f)]$$

The base case are: $eggDrops(1, n) = n$ because if we have only one egg then we have no other option but to climb the floors one by one, and $eggDrops(k, 1) = 1$ because if we have only one floor then we just need to check it. In addition, we can define $eggDrops(k, 0) = 0$ and $eggDrops(0, n) = 0$ because those are borderline cases.

This characterization leads to a straightforward recursion implementation given below where we memorize partial solutions in a support $table$ for avoiding the recompute those solutions again and again.

Code

```
int eggDropHelper(unsigned int k, unsigned int n,
    Matrix<int> & table)
{
    if (n == 1 || n == 0)
        return n;

    if (k == 1)
        return n;

    if (!k)
        return 0;

    unsigned int min =
        std::numeric_limits<unsigned int>::max();
    unsigned int res;

    for (unsigned int f = 1; f <= n; ++f)
    {
        res = std::max(
            ((table(k - 1, f - 1) == -1) ?
                table(k - 1, f - 1) =
                    eggDropHelper(k - 1, f - 1, table) :
                table(k - 1, f - 1)
```

```
                   ),

             (table(k, n - f) == -1) ?
                 table(k, n - f) =
                     eggDropHelper(k, n - f, table) :
                 table(k, n - f)
                 );

        if (res < min)
            min = res;
    }
    return min + 1;
}

int eggDrop(unsigned int k, unsigned int n)
{
    Matrix<int> table(k+1, n+1, -1);
    return eggDropHelper(k, n, table);
}
```

Complexity

The DP solution is left as exercise. A straightforward implementation needs $n * m$ entries in a table where each entry is computed at most n times. Therefore, the algorithm runs in $O(n^2 m)$ time. Time complexity can be reduced to $O(nm)$, if we consider that the optimal floor f for (k, n) is certainly equal or larger than the one for $(k, n - 1)$, so we can avoid to restart the minimum computation from 1. Also, it could be useful to prove that the function $max(eggDrops(k - 1, f - 1), eggDrops(k, n - f)]$ is convex in f so the minimum is unique and can be computed with a linear scan.

9. Jump Stairs – There is a stair with *n* steps. You can climb either one step or two steps at a time. How many different ways there are to climb the stair?

Solution

Let's try a number of examples: If we have only one step, then there is only a way to climb the stair; if we have two steps, then there are two ways (e.g. 1 step, 1 step, or 2 steps); if we have three steps, then there are three ways. More examples are given in the following table:

Steps	#Confs	Configurations
1	1	1
2	2	(1, 1); (2)
3	3	(1, 1, 1); (1, 2) ; (2, 1)
4	5	(1, 1, 1, 1); (2, 1, 1); (1, 2, 1); (1, 1, 2); (2, 2)
5	8	(1, 1, 1, 1, 1); (2, 1, 1, 1); (1, 2, 1, 1); (1, 1, 2, 1); (1, 1, 1, 2); (2, 2, 1); (1, 2, 2), (2, 1, 2)

We notice that there is a pattern: at each step the number of configurations is the sum of the number of configurations of the previous and last steps but one. Mathematically:

$$f(n) = \begin{cases} 1 & n = 1 \\ 2 & n = 2 \\ f(n-1) + f(n-2) & n \geq 2 \end{cases}$$

This formula has a straightforward interpretation: we jump to the n step either from the $n-1$ step or from the $n-2$ step. Note that the base cases are different with respect to Fibonacci.

Code

```
unsigned long jump(unsigned int n)
{
  if (n == 1) return 1;
  if (n == 2) return 2;

  unsigned long current = 0, prev = 2, prevPrev = 1;
  for (unsigned int i = 3; i <= n; i++)
  {
    current = prev + prevPrev;
    prevPrev = prev;
```

```
    prev = current;
  }
  return current;
}
```

Complexity

Linear in the input size.

10.Jumping Array – Given an array of non-negative numbers, start at the first element and reach the end with a minimum number of jumps. A jump cannot exceed the length contained in the current position.

Solution

Given the array $A[0,...n - 1]$, the base cases are when $n - 1 = 0$ or when $A[0] = 0$. For those cases, we have no solution. Otherwise, the mathematical formulation can be computed for each position i by finding the maximum jump length for position $j < i$ such that the required constrain $A[j] \geq (i - j)$ is not violated. Mathematically $jump(i) = max_{j < i} jump(j) + 1 \ if \ A[j] \geq (i - j)$.

Code

```
unsigned int jump(const unsigned int a[], unsigned int n)
{
    std::vector<unsigned int> result(n);
    if (n == 0 || a[0] == 0)
        return std::numeric_limits<unsigned int>::max();

    result[0] = 0;
    for (unsigned int i = 1; i < n; ++i)
    {
        result[i] =
                std::numeric_limits<unsigned int>::max();
        for (unsigned int j = 0; j < i; j++)
        if ((a[j] >= (i - j)) &&
                    (result[j] + 1 < result[i]))
            result[i] = result[j] + 1;
    }
```

21

```
        return result[n - 1];
    }
```

Complexity

Linear in time and space

11.Dice -- Given n dice, count how many ways to get sum s.

Solution

Let's suppose that each die has m faces and define a function $sum(n, m, s)$ which counts how many ways we have to get sum s for n dices with m faces. We can compute this function starting from the result with $n-1$ dices. In particular, if we get a sum $s-i$ from $n-1$ dice we need to add i from the nth die for each $1 \leq i < m$:

$$sum(s,n,m) = sum(s-1, n-1,m) + .. + sum(s-m,n-1, m), \ \ n \geq 2$$

Note that we have $s-m$ terms in this sum. We use a support table mem where we store the current sum and the current dice. The base case is with only one die and in this case there is only one way to get the sum s therefore $mem(i, 1) = 1$ for $1 \leq i < min(m, s)$. Then, for each possible sum value $1 \leq i < s$ and for each possible dice $2 \leq j \leq n$ and for each possible valid value produced by a die $1 < k \leq min(m, i)$ we update mem according to the above definition.

Code

```
unsigned long playDices(unsigned int n, unsigned int m,
unsigned int s)
{
  if ((n == 0) ||  (m < 2) || (s == 0) || (n*m < s) )
    return 0;

  Matrix<int> mem(s + 1, n + 1, 0);
  for (unsigned i = 1; i <= m && i <= s; ++i)
    mem(i, 1) = 1;
```

```
    for (unsigned i = 1; i <= s; ++i)
        for (unsigned j = 2; j <= n; ++j)
            for (unsigned k = 1; k <= m && k < i; ++k)
                mem(i, j) += mem(i - k, j - 1);

    return mem(s, n);
}
```

Complexity

Complexity is $O(nsm)$

12. Coin Change – Given n dollars, how many different ways there are to make the change into a set of coins S?

Solution

Let's define $S = \{s_1, ... s_t\}$ and let $change(n, t)$ be the change for n dollars given a set S of t coins. We suppose to a have an infinite amount of each type of coin s_i. A coin s_i can either be part of the change or not. This simple observation is used for a dynamic programming solution

$$change(n, t) = change(n, t - 1) + change(n - s_t, t)$$

where $change(n, t - 1)$ counts when the coin s_t has been not selected, while $change(n - s_i, t)$ counts the selection of a new coin s_i. The base cases are for $change(0, t) = 1$ where the only solution is not to change any money, $change(n, t) = 0$ for $n < 0$ where there is no solution because we have a negative amount of money, and $change(n, t) = 0$ $t <= 0, N > 0$ because we have money but there is no change available. The first implementation is recursive, while the second is based on dynamic programming.

Code

```
    int changeCoin(int n, const unsigned int S[], int t)
    {
```

```
    if (n == 0)
      return 1;
    if ((n<0) || (t < 0 && n > 0))
      return 0;

    return changeCoin(n, S, t - 1)
      + changeCoin(n - S[t], S, t);
  }


  int changeCoinDP(unsigned int n, const unsigned int S[],
      unsigned int t)
  {
      Matrix<unsigned int> table(n + 1, t);
      for (unsigned int j = 0; j < t; ++j)
          table(0, j) = 1;

      for (unsigned int i = 1; i <= n; ++i)
          for (unsigned int j = 0; j < t; ++j)
              table(i, j) =
                  ((i >= S[j]) ? table(i - S[j], j) : 0) +
                  ((j>0) ? table(i, j - 1) : 0);

      return table(n, t-1);
  }
```

Complexity

Time complexity is $O(nt)$

13. Longest Palindrome String – Given a string, compute the longest palindromic substring

A string is palindromic if it is read the same backward and forward, as *Madam, I'm Adam* or *Poor Dan is in a droop.*

Solution

A solution can be computed for the string $S[0, .., n-1]$ by considering that $LPS(S[0]) = 0$ and

$$LPS(S[0..n-1]) = \begin{cases} LPS(S[1,..n-2]) + 2 & S[0] == S[n-1] \\ max(LPS(S[1,n-1]), LPS(S[0,n-2])) & o.w. \end{cases}$$

This definition computes the longest palindromic substring by starting from the whole string $S[0, .., n-1]$ and it is easy to directly write the code implementing this recursive formulation.

However, another more convenient approach is to define $P[i, j] = true$ if the string is palindromic for $0 \leq i \leq j < n$. The following base cases hold for single characters and for couple of characters:

$$P[i,j] = \begin{cases} true & i = j \\ true & S[i] = S[i+1], \ 0 \leq i < n - 1 \end{cases}$$

In addition, we can define the recurrence $P[i,j] = (P[i+1, j-1] \ and \ S[i] = S[j])$ for increasing lengths $3 \leq len \leq n$ where $0 \leq i \leq n - len + 1$ and $j = i + len - 1$.

Note that with this definition the interval $[i+1, j-1]$ is contained in the interval $[i, j]$ and therefore we just need to test the two characters in the border $(S[i], S[j])$. The code keep tracks of the starting position where the palindromic string begins *longestStart* and its length *maxLen.*.

Code

```cpp
std::string longestPalindrome(const std::string & s) {
    unsigned int n = s.length();
    if (n == 0)
        return s;

    unsigned int longestStart= 0;
    unsigned int maxLen = 1;
    Matrix<unsigned int> table(n, n, false);

    for (unsigned int i = 0; i < n; ++i)
        table(i, i) = true;

    for (unsigned int i = 0; i < n - 1; ++i) {
        if (s[i] == s[i + 1]) {
            table(i, i + 1) = true;
            longestStart = i;
            maxLen = 2;
        }
    }
```

```
    for (unsigned int len = 3; len <= n; ++len) {
        for (unsigned int i = 0; i < n - len + 1; ++i) {
            unsigned int j = i + len - 1;
            if (table(i + 1, j - 1) && s[i] == s[j])
            {
                table(i, j) = true;

                if (len > maxLen)
                {
                    longestStart = i;
                    maxLen = len;
                }
            }
        }
    }
    return s.substr(longestStart, maxLen);
}
```

Complexity

Complexity is $O(n^2)$ and space is $O(n^2)$. Providing a solution with reduced space is left as exercise.

14. String Palindromes -— Given a string, find the minimum number of characters to be inserted for converting the string into a palindrome

Solution

Consider the string $S[l..r]$ and define $num(S[l..r])$ as the number of characters to be inserted for getting a palindrome. We have:

$$num(S[l..r]) = \begin{cases} num(S[l+1...r-1]) & if\ S[l] = S[r] \\ \min\left(num(S[l+1..r]), num(S[l..r-1])\right) + 1 & o.w. \end{cases}$$

The base case are $num(S[l]) = 0$ if $len(S) = 1$ and

$$num(S[l..l+1]) = \begin{cases} 0 & S[l] = S[l+1] \\ 1 & ow \end{cases}$$

A dynamic programming implementation can be realized by adopting a $table(i,j)$ which stores the minimum number of insertions needed to convert $S[l..r]$ into a palindrome. The table is filled in by incremental gap such that $1 \leq gap \leq n$ and by considering the subintervals contained between the positions $[left = 0, right = gap]$, $[left = 1, right = gap + 1], ...,[left = n - gap, right = n]$

Code

```cpp
unsigned int numInsertionPaly(const std::string & str,
    unsigned int l, unsigned int r)
{
    if (r <= l)
        return 0;
    if (l == r - 1)
        return (str[l] == str[r]) ? 0 : 1;

    if (str[l] == str[r])
        return numInsertionPaly(str, l + 1, r - 1);
    else
        return (std::min(numInsertionPaly(str, l + 1, r),
            numInsertionPaly(str, l, r - 1)) + 1);
}

int minInsertionsPalyndromeDP(const std::string & str)
{
    unsigned int n = str.length();
    Matrix<unsigned int> table(n + 1, n + 1, 0);

    unsigned int gap, left, right;
    for (gap = 1; gap < n; ++gap)
        for (left = 0, right = gap;
            right < n; ++left, ++right)
            table(left, right) =
            (str[left] == str[right]) ?
                table(left + 1, right - 1) :
                (std::min(table(left, right - 1),
                    table(left + 1, right)) + 1);

    return table(0, n - 1);
}
```

Complexity

Complexity is $O(n^2)$ in time and space

15.LCS -- Given two strings *S1* and i, find the longest common substring

The longest common substring problem consists in finding the longest string that is a substring of two strings.[3]

Solution

On way to solve the problem is to find the longest common suffix for all the pairs of prefixes for the strings $S1$ and S2. The longest common suffix is:

$$LCSuf(S1_{1,m}, S2_{1,n}) = \begin{cases} LCSuf(S1_{1,m-1}, S2_{1,n-1}) + 1 & S1[m] = S2[n] \\ 0 & o.w. \end{cases}$$

Given $LCSuf$, we can compute the longest common substring because the maximal of the longest common suffixes of all possible prefixes is the longest common substring of S1 and T1.

$$LCSubstring(S1, S2,) =$$

$$max\ (LCSuf(S1_{1,..i}, S2_{1...j}), 0 < i \le m, 0 < j \le n$$

Code

```cpp
int LCSubStr(const std::string & S1, const std::string & S2)
{
  unsigned int m = S1.length();
  unsigned int n = S2.length();
  unsigned int result = 0;

  Matrix<unsigned int> LCSuff(m + 1, n + 1);

  for (unsigned int i = 0; i <= m; i++) {
    for (unsigned int j = 0; j <= n; j++) {
      if (i == 0 || j == 0) {
        LCSuff(i, j) = 0;
      } else if (S1[i - 1] == S2[j - 1]) {
        result = std::max(
```

---

[3] http://en.wikipedia.org/wiki/Longest_common_substring_problem

```
        (LCSuff(i, j) = LCSuff(i - 1, j - 1) + 1),
        result
      );
  } else {
    LCSuff(i, j) = 0;
  }
 }
}
return result;
}
```

Complexity

Complexity is $O(nm)$ and space is $O(nm)$. Reducing the space to $O(min(n, m))$ is left as an exercise.

16. LCS – Given two strings, find the longest common subsequence

Given the two strings, two subsequences are in common if they appear in the same order but not necessarily contiguous. The main difference with the previous problem is that here the terms are not consecutive.

Solution

A dynamic programming solution can be computed for the string $S1[0, .., n - 1]$ and the string $S2[0, .., m - 1]$ by defining a recursive function $LCS(S1_i, S2_j)$ on the prefixes $S1_i$ and $S2_j$ of length i and j

$$LCS(S1_i, S2_j) = \begin{cases} 0 & i = 0 \; or \; j = 0 \\ LCS(S1_{i-1}, S2_{j-1}) + 1 & S1[i] = S2[j] \\ max(LCS(S1_{i-1}, S2_j), LCS(S1_i, S2_{j-1})) & ow \end{cases}$$

A dynamic programming solution can be built by using a table where we store the partial results of the above computation (function LCS). In addition we store the direction that generated the table for reconstructing the common subsequence in a next step (function $printLCS$)

Code

```cpp
enum where{DiagonalUpward, Upward, Downward};

void printLCS(const Matrix<where>& directions, const
std::string& str,
     unsigned int i, unsigned int j)
{
 if (i == 0 || j == 0)return;
 if (directions(i, j) == DiagonalUpward)
 {
     printLCS(directions, str, i - 1, j - 1);
     std::cout << str[i];
 }
 else if (directions(i, j) == Upward)
     printLCS(directions, str, i - 1, j);
 else
     printLCS(directions, str, i, j - 1);
}

void LCS(const std::string& s1, const std::string& s2)
{
 const unsigned int m = s1.size() + 1;
 const unsigned int n = s2.size() + 1;

 Matrix<unsigned int> table(m, n, 0);
 Matrix<where> directions(m, n);

 for (unsigned int i = 1; i<m; i++)
     for (unsigned int j = 1; j<n; j++)
         if (s1[i] == s2[j])
         {
             table(i, j) = table(i - 1, j - 1) + 1;
             directions(i, j) = DiagonalUpward;
         }
         else
             if (table(i - 1,j) >= table(i, j - 1))
             {
                 table(i, j) = table(i - 1, j);
                 directions(i, j) = Upward;
             }
             else
             {
                 table(i, j) = table(i, j - 1);
                 directions(i, j) = Downward;
             }

             printLCS(directions, s1, m-1, n-1);
}
```

Complexity

Complexity is $O(nm)$ and space is $O(nm)$.

17.LIS – Given an array of integers, find the longest increasing subsequence

Solution

The solution can be quickly identified by dynamic programming. Suppose that we scan the array A, then at position i we have that

$$LSI(A[i]) = \begin{cases} 1 + Max(LSI(j)) & j < i \ \&\& \ A[j] < A[i] \\ 1 & otherwise \end{cases}$$

Code

```cpp
unsigned int LIS(const std::vector<unsigned int> & v)
{
    unsigned int max;
    unsigned int n = v.size();
    std::vector<unsigned int> maxHere(n, 0);

    for (unsigned int k = 0; k < n; ++k)
    {
        max = 0;
        for (unsigned int j = 0; j < k; ++j)
            if (v[k] > v[j])
                if (maxHere[j] > max)
                    max = maxHere[j];
        maxHere[k] = max + 1;
    }
    max = 0;
    for (unsigned int k = 0; k < n; ++k)
        if (maxHere[k] > max)
            max = maxHere[k];

    return max;
}
```

Complexity

Complexity is $O(n^2)$ and space is $O(n)$. An $O(nlogn)$ algorithm is

31

described here[4].

18. Bridge Matching – n cities are on the northern bank of a river and n cities are on the southern bank. You can build a bridge only between cities with the same number

Solution

Let $N(i)$ be the number of cities i on the northern bank and $S(i)$ the number of cities j on the southern bank. The problem can be reduced to the one of finding the longest common subsequence. Suppose to sort the bridges built by their first city. If two bridges cross, then we have one bridge (n_i, s_i) and another bridge (n_j, s_j) such that either $n_i < n_j$ and $s_i > s_j$ or $n_i > n_j$ and $s_i < s_j$. We can sort the tuples by increasing n_i indexes and then compute the longest increasing sequence (LIS) on the sequence of s_i.

Code

Left as exercise

Complexity

Since we need to sort the complexity is $O(n \log n)$

19. LBS – Given an array of integers, find the longest bitonic sequence

Solution

A sequence is bitonic, if it initially increases and then decreases. For an array A we can compute the longest increasing sequence $LSI(A[i])$ ending

---

[4] http://en.wikipedia.org/wiki/Longest_increasing_subsequence

at position i and the longest decreasing sequence $LSD(A[i])$ starting at position i. For each position i we define:

$$bitonic(A[i]) = LSI(A[i]) + LSD(A[i]) - 1$$

and

$$bitonic(A) = max_i(bitonic(A[i]))$$

Code

Left as exercise

Complexity

Complexity is $O(nlogn)$.

20.Box Stacking – Given a set of *3d* boxes, compute the largest stack of boxes. A box can be stacked only on top of another box with larger base.

Solution

This problem is a variation of the longest increasing sequence. Each box i has three dimensions $height(i)$, $width(i)$, $depth(i)$ which can be rotated to form the base: either $(height(i), width(i))$, or $(depth(i), width(i))$, or $(depth(i), heigth(i))$. If we suppose having infinite amount of each box types, then we can solve this problem by computing the LIS for the remaining dimensions of the box.

Code

Left as exercise

Complexity

Complexity is $O(n^2)$.

21.Sum Subset -– Given an array of integers of size n, partition it in such a way that the two subsets have equal sum s

Solution

Sum subset problem is and important problem in computer science with application in cryptography and complexity[5]. The problem is NP-Complete. The most naïve solution generates all the subsets and for each of them it checks whether the sum is the right number. The complexity is $O(n2^n)$ where n the size of the array.

We can use Dynamic programming for providing a pseudo-polynomial solution. First, if the sum is odd there is no solution, while if the sum is even we can try to find a subset. Second, if the current element is larger than the sum we must skip it, otherwise we can decide whether we want to include it or not. Therefore $sb(i,j)$ depends on $sb(i,j-1)$, if we don't include the element $v[j-1]$ for the position $0 < j < n$ and for the current sum value $0 < i < s$. While it depends on $sb(v, i - v[j-1], j-1)$ if we include the element.

$$sb(i,j) = \begin{cases} sb(i, j-1) & 0 < i < s, 0 < j < n \\ sb(i, j-1) || sb(i - v[j-1], j-1) & 0 < i < s, 0 < j < n, i > v[j-1] \end{cases}$$

The base cases are $sub(0,j) = true$ because there is always a subset with zero sum, and $sub(i,0) = false$ because the empty set cannot have a subset of sum i. The code implements a recursive and a dynamic programming solution

Code

```
bool isSubsetSum(const std::vector<unsigned int> & v,
    const unsigned int n, unsigned int sum)
{
    if (n == 0 && sum != 0)
```

---

[5] http://en.wikipedia.org/wiki/Subset_sum_problem

```cpp
        return false;
    if (sum == 0)
        return true;
    if (v[n - 1] > sum)
        return isSubsetSum(v, n - 1, sum);
    return isSubsetSum(v, n - 1, sum) ||
        isSubsetSum(v, n - 1, sum - v[n - 1]);
}

bool partition(const std::vector<unsigned int> & v,
    unsigned int n)
{
    int sum = std::accumulate(v.begin(), v.end(), 0);
    if (sum % 2 != 0)
        return false;
    return isSubsetSum(v, n, sum / 2);
}

bool isSubsetSumDP(const std::vector<unsigned int> & v,
    const unsigned int n, unsigned int sum)
{
    Matrix<bool> subset(sum + 1, n + 1);

    for (unsigned int j = 0; j <= n; j++)
        subset(0, j) = true;

    for (unsigned int i = 1; i <= sum; i++)
        subset(i, 0) = false;

    for (unsigned int i = 1; i <= sum; i++)
    for (unsigned int j = 1; j <= n; j++) {
        subset(i, j) = subset(i, j - 1);
        if (i >= v[j - 1]) {
            subset(i, j) = subset(i, j) ||
                subset(i - v[j - 1], j - 1);
        }
    }
    return subset(sum, n);
}
```

Complexity

Complexity is pseudo-polynomial $O(ns)$

22. Partition Set – partition a multiset S of positive integers into two subsets *S1* and *S2*, such that the sum of the numbers in *S1* equals the sum of the numbers in *S2*

Solution

This is a variant of the previous problem with a similar pseudo linear solution based on dynamic programming.

Code

```cpp
bool isPartitionDP(const std::vector<unsigned int> & v)
{
  unsigned int sum = std::accumulate(v.begin(), v.end(), 0);
  return isSubsetSumDP(v, v.size(), sum / 2);
}

void testPartition()
{
  int v1[] = { 3, 1, 1, 2, 2, 1 };
  std::vector<unsigned int> vec1(v1,
    v1 + sizeof(v1) / sizeof(int));
  if (isPartitionDP(vec1) == true)
    std::cout << "Found a partition";
  else
    std::cout << "No partition";
}
```

Complexity

Complexity is pseudo-polynomial $O(ns)$, where sum is the sum of elements in the vector.

23. Segment Partition -– Given a segment of integer length *n,* cut it into different integer parts in such a way to maximize the product of the lengths of all parts.

Solution

We can split the segment for all the integer positions and compute the max product of the two parts. If we split it in position i, then the product is $i * (n - i)$. In addition, the part $(n - i)$ can be further split. So the product can be reclusively computed as $prod(n) = \max\ (i * (n - i),\ i * prod(n - i))\ for\ 1 \le i \le n$. The base cases are $prod(0) = 1,\ prod(1) = 0$.

Code

```cpp
unsigned int segment(unsigned int n)
{
    if (n == 0 || n == 1) return 0;

    unsigned int m = 0;
    for (unsigned int i = 1; i < n; i++)
        m = std::max(m, std::max(i * (n - i),
            segment(n - i) * i));

    return m;
}

unsigned int segmentDPhelper(unsigned int n,
    std::vector<unsigned int> & seg)
{
    unsigned int m = 0;
    for (unsigned int i = 1; i < n; i++)
    {
        if (!seg[n - i])
            seg[n - i] = segmentDPhelper(n - i, seg);
        m = std::max(m, std::max(i * (n - i),
                            seg[n - i] * i));
    }
    return m;
}
```

37

```
unsigned int segmentDP(unsigned int n)
{
    if (n == 0 || n == 1) return 0;
    std::vector<unsigned int> seg(n, 0);
    return segmentDPhelper(n, seg);
}
```

Complexity

Linear in time and space

24. Cutting a Rod – given a rod of length n and a vector of prices for different lengths, cut the rod for maximizing the gain

Solution

The idea is very similar to the one of the previous problem. Let's suppose to have an array of $prices[i]$ we can define

$cut(n) = max(price[i] + cut(n - i - 1))$ for $0 <= i < n$

Code

```
unsigned int cutDPhelper(
    const std::vector<unsigned int> & price,
    unsigned int n, std::vector<unsigned int> & cut)
{
    unsigned int m = 0;
    for (unsigned int i = 1; i < n; i++)
    {
        if (!cut[n - i - 1])
            cut[n - i - 1] =
                cutDPhelper(price, n - i - 1, cut);
        m = std::max(m, price[i] + cut[n - i - 1]);
    }
    return m;
}

unsigned int cutDP(const std::vector<unsigned int> & price,
    unsigned int n)
{
```

```
    if (n <= 0) return 0;
    std::vector<unsigned int> seg(n, 0);
    return cutDPhelper(price, n, seg);
}
```

Complexity

Linear in time and space.

25.Bellman-Ford – Given a graph *G* and a source vertex, find the shortest paths from the source *src* to all vertices. The graph may contain negative edges

Solution

This is a classical dynamic programming problem and the solution is due to Bellman-Ford[6]. Let's suppose that $weight(u,v)$ is the weight associated to the $edge\ (u, v)$ for each edge in a directed graph $G = (V, E)$. For our computation we need a support array $dist[]$ of size $|V|$. The first step is to initialize all entries in $dist[]$ to infinite with the only exception of $dist[src] = 0$ because src is reachable with zero distance. Then, for $|V| - 1$ times we compute:

$$for\ each\ edge\ (u, v)$$

$$if\ (dist[v] > dist[u] + weight(u, v))$$

$$dist[v] = dist[u] + weight(u, v)$$

At the end a negative edge can be detected by checking for each edge whether(u, v), if $dist[v] > dist[u] + weight(u, v)$

Code

```
void BellmanFord(const Graph & g, int src)
```

---

[6] http://en.wikipedia.org/wiki/Bellman-Ford_algorithm

```
{
  std::vector<int> dist(g.numNodes(),
          std::numeric_limits<int>::max());
  std::vector<int> predecessor(g.numNodes(), -1);

  dist[src] = 0;

  for (nodeID u = 0; u < g.numNodes(); u++)
      for (auto const & e : g.edges(u))
      {
          if (dist[u] + e.w < dist[e.v])
          {
              dist[e.v] = dist[u] + e.w;
              predecessor[e.v] = u;
          }
      }

  for (nodeID u = 0; u < g.numNodes(); u++)
      for (auto const & e : g.edges(u))
          if (dist[u] + e.w < dist[e.v])
              std::cout << "negative cycle";

  for (nodeID v = 0; v < g.numNodes(); ++v)
      std::cout << predecessor[v] << "->"
          << v << " d=" << dist[v] << std::endl;
}
```

Complexity

Time complexity is $O(V\,E)$

26. Max Submatrix 0/1 - Given a matrix consisting only of 0s and 1s, find the maximum size square sub-matrix with all 1s

Solution

A dynamic programming solution can be defined as follows. Let M be the matrix of 0s and 1s of size $(n * m)$ and consider another matrix S of same size. If $M[i][j] = 1$, then it can contribute to either position $S[i-1][j]$, or $S[i][j-1]$, or $S[i-1][j-1]$ which can be expressed as $S[i][j] = min(S[i][j-1], S[i-1][j], S[i-1][j-1]) + 1$. If $M[i][j] = 0$ then

$S[i][j] = 0$. Here is the code

Code

```cpp
void FindMaxSubSquare(const Matrix<bool> & m,
    int &maxI, int &maxJ, int &size)
{
Matrix<int> s(m.dim1(), m.dim2());

for (unsigned i = 0; i < m.dim1(); i++)
    s(i, 0) = m(i, 0);

for (unsigned j = 0; j < m.dim2(); j++)
    s(0, j) = m(0, j);

for (unsigned int i = 1; i < m.dim1(); i++)
    for (unsigned int j = 1; j < m.dim2(); j++)
    {
        if (m(i,j))
            s(i,j) = std::min(std::min(s(i,j - 1),
                s(i - 1, j)), s(i - 1,j - 1)) + 1;
        else
            s(i, j) = 0;
    }

size = s(0, 0); maxI = 0; maxJ = 0;
for (unsigned int i = 0; i < m.dim1(); i++)
    for (unsigned int j = 0; j < m.dim2(); j++)
        if (size < s(i, j))
        {
            size = s(i, j);
            maxI = i;
            maxJ = j;
        }
}
```

Complexity

Complexity is $O(n\,m)$

27.Matrix Parenthesization -- Given a set of *m* Matrices find the most efficient way of multiplying them

Solution

Matrix multiplication is associative so there are multiple ways of performing the multiplication and therefore the number of operations (sum and multiplications) performed on scalars is different. Let's suppose that the dimensions of the ith matrix is contained in positions $(p[i-1], p[i])$ for a vector $p[0, m-1]$. We can scan the vector and find a solution recursively.

Code

```cpp
unsigned int MatrixOrder(const std::vector<unsigned int>&p,
        int i, int j)
{
    if (i == j)
        return 0;

    unsigned int min =
        std::numeric_limits<unsigned int>::max();
    unsigned int res;

    for (int k = i; k <j; ++k)
    {
        res = MatrixOrder(p, i, k) +
            MatrixOrder(p, k + 1, j) +
            p[i - 1] * p[k] * p[j];

        if (res < min)
            min = res;
    }
    return min;
}

unsigned int MatrixChainOrder(const std::vector<unsigned
int> & p)
{
    unsigned int n = p.size();
```

```
Matrix<unsigned int> m(n, n);

for (unsigned int i = 0; i < n; ++i)
    m(i, i) = 0;

unsigned int j, cost;

// len = 2,   1 <= i < n - 1 ; j = i + 1
// len = 3,   1 <= i < n - 2;  j = i + 2
//
// len = n-2, i=1, i = 2 , j = i + n - 3
// len = n-1, i=1          , j = n - 1

for (unsigned int len = 2; len < n; ++len)
    for (unsigned i = 1; i < n - len + 1; ++i)
    {
        j = i + len - 1;
        m(i, j) =
            std::numeric_limits<unsigned int>::max();
        for (unsigned int k = i; k <= j - 1; ++k)
        {
            cost = m(i, k) + m(k + 1, j) +
                p[i - 1] * p[k] * p[j];
            if (cost < m(i, j)) {
                m(i, j) = cost;
            }
        }
    }
    return m(1, n - 1);
}
```

Complexity

Complexity is $O(m^3)$

28. Max Submatrix – Given a matrix of size $n \times n$ find the maximum sum rectangle

Solution

The problem is a natural generalization of the Kandane's problem discussed previously. Suppose that we fix columns i and j, then we can compute in linear time the top and bottom rows which maximize the rectangle.

Code

```cpp
void findMaxSum(const Matrix<int> & M)
{
    unsigned int rows = M.dim1();
    unsigned int columns = M.dim2();
    unsigned int finalLeft, finalRight, finalUp, finalDown;
    int sum, start, stop, maxSum =
std::numeric_limits<int>::min();

    for (unsigned int left = 0; left < columns; ++left)
    {
        std::vector<int> temp(rows, 0);
        for (unsigned int right = left; right < columns;
++right)
        {
            for (unsigned int i = 0; i <rows; ++i)
                temp[i] += M(i, right);

            sum = kadane(temp, start, stop);

            if (sum > maxSum)
            {
                maxSum = sum;
                finalLeft = left; finalRight = right;
                finalUp = start; finalDown = stop;
            }
        }
    }
    std::cout << "maxSum=" << maxSum <<
        " (Top, Left) (" << finalUp <<
        " ," << finalLeft <<
        ") (Bottom, Right) (" << finalDown <<
        "," << finalRight << ')' << std::endl;
}
```

Complexity

Complexity is (n^3), because Kandane is linear.

29. Given a Binary Search Tree, find the size of the largest independent set of nodes

Solution

A set of nodes in a tree is independent if there are no edges directly connecting them in a father-children relation. A dynamic programming solution is based on the consideration that a node can be either part of the largest independent set or not. In the former case the size of the largest set will be the sum of the largest set of grandchildren plus 1 because we skip the grandchildren's father. In the latter case the size of the largest set is the sum of the largest set of children because by construction we do not add any new node to the set. Formally:

$$LIS(n) = MAX \left(\left(\sum_{x \in grandchildren(n)} LIS(x) \right) + 1, \sum_{x \in children(n)} LIS(x) \right)$$

If a node is null then $LIS(NULL) = 0$. For avoiding re-computing partial results we can store the LIS(x) inside the node X.

Code

```cpp
template <typename T>
struct node
{
    T value;
    mutable unsigned int liss;
    struct node* left, *right;
    node(T v) : value(v), liss(0), left(NULL), right(NULL)
{};
};

template <typename T>
unsigned int LargestIndipendentSet(const node<T> * root)
{
    if (root == NULL)
        return 0;

    if (root->liss)
        return root->liss;
```

```
    unsigned int sizeWithThisNode = 1;

    if (root->left)
        sizeWithThisNode +=
        LargestIndipendentSet(root->left->left) +
        LargestIndipendentSet(root->left->right);

    if (root->right)
        sizeWithThisNode +=
        LargestIndipendentSet(root->right->left) +
        LargestIndipendentSet(root->right->right);

    unsigned int sizeWithoutThisNode =
        LargestIndipendentSet(root->right) +
        LargestIndipendentSet(root->left);

    root->liss = std::max(sizeWithThisNode,
        sizeWithoutThisNode);
    return root->liss;
}
```

Complexity

The total complexity is $O(n)$ where n is the number of nodes in the binary search tree.

30. Optimal Binary Tree – given a set *S* of tuples *<k, freq[k]>* , where *k* is an integer and *freq[k]* is the number of times that *k* has been observed, build a binary search three such that the total cost of all single searches is minimized

Solution

One key intuition is that the cost of accessing a key is $[k] * depth[k]$, where $depth[k]$ is the depth of key k. A tuple can be the root of the binary search tree (BST) provided that it respects the BST properties:

- The left subtree of a node contains only nodes with keys less than the node's key

- The right subtree of a node contains only nodes with keys greater than the node's key

- For the left and right subtree: each one must also be a binary search tree

- There must be no duplicate nodes

Therefore we can write the cost function for the keys in (i, j) as it follows:

$$cost(i, j) = \sum_{k=i}^{j} freq[k] + min_{r=i}^{j} [cost(i, r-1), cost(r+1, j)]$$

In other words: when the node $0 \leq r < n$ becomes a root and we need to minimize the cost of the left keys $[0, ..., r)$ and the right keys $(r, ..., n)$. In addition, all the nodes below the new root node will have an additional level of depth and therefore we need to sum all their frequencies. The code provided uses memorization for avoiding recomputation of the same values again and again. The solution is built bottom-up.

Code

```cpp
int costBST_DP(const std::vector<unsigned int> & freq)
{
    unsigned int n = freq.size();
    Matrix<unsigned int> cost(n, n);
    Matrix<unsigned int> sumFreq(n, n);
    unsigned int localCost;

    for (unsigned int i = 0; i < n; ++i)
        cost(i, i) = freq[i];

    for (unsigned int i = 0; i < n; ++i)
    for (unsigned int j = i; j < n; ++j)
    {
        sumFreq(i, j) = 0;
        for (unsigned int s = i; s <= j && s < n; ++s)
            sumFreq(i, j) += freq[s];
    }
    // range = 2 (0<=i<n-1) -> j=i+1 1<=j<=n-1
    // range = 3 (0<=i<n-2) -> j=i+2 0<=j<=n-1
    // range = n (i=0) -> j = n-1

    for (unsigned int range = 2; range <= n; ++range)
```

```
      for (unsigned int i = 0; i < n - range + 1; ++i)
      {
          unsigned int j = i + range - 1;
          cost(i, j) = std::numeric_limits<unsigned
  int>::max();

          for (unsigned int k = i; k <= j; k++)
          {
              localCost =
                  ((k > i) ? cost(i, k - 1) : 0) +
                  ((k < j) ? cost(k + 1, j) : 0) + sumFreq(i,
  j);
              if (localCost < cost(i, j))
                  cost(i, j) = localCost;
          }
      }
      return cost(0, n - 1);
  }
```

Complexity

The cost is $O(n^3)$ and space is $O(n^2)$

31. Boolean Parenthesization – given a Boolean expression of and, or, xor, true, false, find the number of ways to parenthesize and evaluate to true

Solution

Let $T(i,j)$ be the number of parenthesizations which are evaluated to true between positions i and j; and $F(i,j)$ be the number of parenthesization which are evaluated to false between positions i and j. Recursively

$$T(i,j) = \begin{cases} T(i,k)T(k+1,j) & op = AND \\ (T(i,k) + F(i,k))(T(k+1,j) + F(k+1,j)) - F(i,k)F(k+1,j) & op = OR \\ T(i,k)F(k+1,j) + F(i,k)T(k+1,j) & op = XOR \end{cases}$$

$$F(i,j) = \begin{cases} (T(i,k) + F(i,k))(T(k+1,j) + F(k+1,j)) - T(i,k)T(k+1,j) & op = AND \\ F(i,k)F(k+1,j) & op = OR \\ T(i,k)F(k+1,j) + F(i,k)T(k+1,j) & op = XOR \end{cases}$$

Code

Left as exercise

Complexity

The running time is $O(n^3)$, where n are the number of items in the expression.

32. Games of Coins – a set of coins are aligned and two players can pick one coin from each side in turn. Maximize the value of the coins picked by the first player

Solution

Let suppose that the coins are represented in an array $c[0, n)$. The value picked when the coins left are $[a, b]$ must satisfy the recursive relation $v(a, b)$:

$$v(a, b) = \begin{cases} \max \begin{array}{l} (c(a) + \min\,(v(a+2, b), v(a+1, b-1)), \\ c(b) + min(v(a, b-2), v(a+1, b-1))) \end{array} & a \le b \\ 0 & a > b \end{cases}$$

The key intuition is that the first player should select either coin a or coin b with the goal of maximizing his gain. For the sake of simplicity, let's suppose he selects a: the other case is symmetric. We count $c(a)$ plus we aim at minimizing the value of the second player who can either pick another coin from the a side (position a+2) or pick a coin from the b side. The value is clearly 0 if $a > b$.

Code

Left as exercise

Complexity

There are $O(n^2)$ values for $[a, b]$ and each single evaluation is $O(1)$, so the total run time is $O(n^2)$

33. Maximum value contiguous subsequence – given an array of real numbers, find a contiguous subsequence with max sum s

Solution

Let's define $M(i)$ as the maximum value subsequence which ends at i. The element in position i can be either added or not. Recursively

$$M(i) = \begin{cases} a_i & i = 0 \\ \max\left(M(i-1)\right) + a_i, a_i\right) & i > 0 \end{cases}$$

Code

Left as exercise

Complexity

There are n elements in M and the computing of each element requires to compute the maximum between two values. Therefore complexity is $O(n)$

34. Balanced partition – given an array of integers between 0 and M, divide the integers into two sets such that the difference of their sums is minimized

Solution

Let $c_{ij} = 1$, if the subset $\{x_1, ..., x_i\}$ sums to j. Recursively for the set of i elements we can start with a set of $i - 1$ elements and keep it as it is, or we can expand it by adding the element x_j

$$c_{ij} = \begin{cases} 1 & i = 0, j = 0 \\ max(c_{i-1,j}, c_{i-1,j-x_j}) & i > 0 \end{cases}$$

Then considering the row c_{nj} representing $\{x_1, ..., x_n\}$ we search the value b

such that $c_{nb} = 1$ and the difference $\left| c_{nb} - \frac{1}{2}\sum_{i}^{n} x_i \right|$ is minimized.

Code

Left as exercise

Complexity

There are n elements bounded by M while j needs to scan n elements. Therefore the complexity is $O(n^2 M)$

35. Scheduling – given n jobs, each one with a processing time ti a profit pi and a deadline di, maximize the profit

Solution

Suppose that each job x_i has processing time t_i profit p_i and deadline d_i for $0 \le i < n$ and that we get no profit, if the job is executed after its deadline. We want to maximize the profit $P(i,j)$ for $0 \le i < n$ jobs executed at time j. Recursively,

$$P(i, j) = \begin{cases} 0 & i = 0 \\ max(P(i - 1, j), \ P(i - 1, j - t_i) + p_i & j \le d_i \\ P(i - 1, j) & o.w. \end{cases}$$

Code

Left as exercise

Complexity

If we assume that the processing time is bounded by M, then we need to compute j up to Mn and we have n jobs to consider. Therefore the total complexity is $O(n^2 M)$

36. Stock prices – Given a histogram array of unsigned integers encoding the price of a stock title during the previous year, compute the area for the largest rectangle contained in this histogram

Solution

Let A be the histogram array, we need to compute

$$max_{j < i}((j - i + 1) * min(\sum_{k = i}^{j} A[k]))$$

The most naïve implementation has complexity $O(n^3)$. However we can achieve complexity $O(n^2)$ by processing each element $0 \leq i < n$ and looking for the largest rectangle with height being at least $A[i]$. Complexity can be further improved by considering that if we have $p < q \leq i$ and $[p] > A[q]$, then we can immediately discard $A[p]$ when processing the ith entry and this can be efficiently achieved by using a stack.

Code

```cpp
unsigned int largestRectangle(
    const std::vector<unsigned int> & H)
{
 std::stack<unsigned int> stk;
 std::vector<unsigned int> left;

 for (unsigned int i = 0; i < H.size(); ++i)
 {
     while (!stk.empty() && H[stk.top()] > H[i])
         stk.pop();
     stk.push(i);
     left.push_back(stk.empty() ? -1 : stk.top());
 }
 while (!stk.empty()) { stk.pop(); }
```

```
std::vector<unsigned int> right(H.size());
for (int i = H.size() - 1; i >= 0; --i)
{
    while (!stk.empty() && H[stk.top()] > H[i])
        stk.pop();
    right[i] = stk.empty() ? H.size() : stk.top();
    stk.push(i);
}

unsigned int maxArea = 0;
for (unsigned int i = 0; i < H.size(); ++i)
{
    maxArea =
        std::max(maxArea, H[i] * (right[i] - left[i] - 1));
}
return maxArea;
}
```

Complexity

Code runs in $O(n^2)$.

37. Ship Battle – Given a matrix M and an array V, match the array in the matrix

Solution

Let M be the matrix of size $n \times m$, and A the array of size l. We can scan the matrix by rows $0 \leq i < n$ and by columns $0 \leq j < m$ and if $M(i,j) = v(l)$, with vector at position $0 \leq l < len$, we can recursively check, if there is a match for the eight positions adjacent to (i, j) with $v(l + 1)$. Particular attention must be put for the corner cases as explained in the code. If we cache the situations where the match does not happen for tuples (i, j, l), we can obtain complexity $O(nml)$

Code

```
// (i, j, k) -> v
typedef Tensor<unsigned int, unsigned int,
    unsigned int, bool> Cache;

bool matchHelper(const Matrix<int> &m,
```

```cpp
                    const std::vector<int> &v,
                    Cache & doNot,
                    int i,
                    int j,
                    unsigned int len)
{
//   std::cout << " matchHelper i=" << i
 << " j=" << j << " len=" << len << std::endl;

 if (v.size() == len)
     return true;

 if (i < 0 || i >= (int)m.dim1() ||
 j < 0 || j >= (int)m.dim2() || doNot.exist(i, j, len))
     return false;

 if ((m(i, j) == v[len]) &&
     (matchHelper(m, v, doNot,
         i - 1, j, len + 1) || /* horizontal */
      matchHelper(m, v, doNot,
         i + 1, j, len + 1) || /* horizontal */
      matchHelper(m, v, doNot,
         i, j - 1, len + 1) || /* vertical */
      matchHelper(m, v, doNot,
         i, j + 1, len + 1) || /* vertical */

      matchHelper(m, v, doNot,
         i - 1, j - 1, len + 1) || /* diagonal */
      matchHelper(m, v, doNot,
         i - 1, j + 1, len + 1) || /* diagonal */
      matchHelper(m, v, doNot,
         i + 1, j - 1, len + 1) || /* diagonal */
      matchHelper(m, v, doNot,
         i + 1, j + 1, len + 1)    /* diagonal */
     ))
     return true;

     doNot(i, j, len) = true;
     return false;
}

bool matchVectorInMatrix(const Matrix<int> & m,
     const std::vector<int> & v)
{
 Cache c;
 for (unsigned int i = 0; i < m.dim1(); ++i)
     for (unsigned int j = 0; j < m.dim2(); ++j)
         if (matchHelper(m, v, c, i, j, 0))
```

```
            return true;

    return false;
    }
```

Complexity

Code runs in $O(nml)$.

Appendix

This appendix contains two support classes defined for solving a certain number of problems

Graph class

```cpp
#include <forward_list>
typedef unsigned int nodeID;
typedef int weight;
struct Edge
{
 nodeID v;
 weight w;

 Edge(nodeID d, weight wt) : v(d), w(wt) {};
};

typedef std::forward_list<Edge> edgesList; // list of edges
leaving a node
typedef std::vector<edgesList> Edges;
class Graph
{
public:
 // allocate |V| lists of edges
 Graph(unsigned int V) : _V(V), _E(0), _edges(new Edges(V))
{};
 ~Graph(){ delete _edges; };

 void addEdge(nodeID v1, nodeID v2, weight w)
 {
     if (v1 > _V || v2 > _V) return;
     Edge e(v2, w);
     (*_edges)[v1].push_front(e);
     _E++;
 }

 void addNode()
 {
     edgesList el;
     _edges->push_back(el);
     _V++;
 }

 edgesList & edges(nodeID v) const { return (*_edges)[v]; };
```

```cpp
unsigned int numNodes() const { return _V; };
unsigned int numEdges() const { return _E; };

private:
 unsigned int _V, _E;
 Edges * _edges;
};

std::ostream & operator << (std::ostream & os,
    const Graph & g)
{
 for (nodeID u = 0; u < g.numNodes(); u++)
 {
    os << " node=" << u << std::endl;
    for (auto const & e : g.edges(u))
        os << " ->" << e.v << " w=" << e.w << std::endl;
 }
 return os;
}
```

Matrix class

```cpp
template<typename T>
class Matrix
{
public:
 Matrix(const Matrix&) = delete;
 Matrix& operator=(const Matrix&) = delete;

 Matrix(unsigned int dim1, unsigned int dim2)
     : _M(new T*[dim1]), _dim1(dim1), _dim2(dim2)
 {
     for (unsigned int i = 0; i < dim1; ++i)
         _M[i] = new T[dim2];
 }
 Matrix(unsigned int dim1, unsigned int dim2,
         T defaultValue)
     : Matrix(dim1, dim2)
 {
     for (unsigned int i = 0; i < _dim1; ++i)
     for (unsigned int j = 0; j < _dim2; ++j)
         _M[i][j] = defaultValue;
 }

 Matrix(Matrix&& aMatrix) {
     _dim1 = aMatrix._dim1;
     _dim2 = aMatrix._dim2;
     _M = aMatrix._M;
     aMatrix._dim1 = 0;
     aMatrix._dim2 = 0;
     aMatrix._M = nullptr;
 }

 ~Matrix()
 {
     for (unsigned int i = 0; i < _dim1; ++i)
         delete[] _M[i];
     delete[] _M;
 }
 T & operator()(const unsigned int i, const unsigned int j)
 {
     return _M[i][j];
 }
```

```cpp
T & operator()(const unsigned int i, const unsigned int j)
const
{
    return _M[i][j];
}

unsigned int dim1() const { return _dim1; };
unsigned int dim2() const { return _dim2; };

friend std::ostream & operator <<(std::ostream & out,
        const Matrix<T>& m)
{
    for (unsigned int i = 0; i < m._dim1; ++i){
        for (unsigned int j = 0; j < m._dim2; ++j)
            out << m._M[i][j] << ' ';
        out << std::endl;
    }
    return out;
}

void swap(Matrix & other)
{
    std::swap(_M, other._M);
    std::swap(_dim1, other._dim1);
    std::swap(_dim2, other._dim2);
}
private:
    T** _M;
    unsigned int _dim1, _dim2;
};
```

Tensor class

```cpp
#include <functional>
#include <unordered_map>
template <typename T1, typename T2, typename T3, typename V>
class Tensor
{
public:
    V & operator()(const T1 i, const T2 j, const T3 k)
    {
        Point p(i, j, k);
        return _M[p];
    }
    V & operator()(const T1 i, const T2 j, const T3 k)const
    {
        Point p(i, j, k);
        return _M[p];
    }

    bool exist(const T1 i, const T2 j, const T3 k) const
    {
        Point p(i, j, k);
        return (_M.find(p) != _M.cend());
    }

    void swap(Tensor<T1, T2, T3, V> & other)
    {
        std::swap(_M, other._M);
    }

    Tensor & operator = (Tensor<T1, T2, T3, V> & other)
    {
        swap(other);
        return *this;
    }

    friend std::ostream & operator <<(std::ostream & out,
        const Tensor<T1, T2, T3, V>& ts)
    {
        for (const auto & p : ts._M)
            std::cout << "(" << p.first.i << "," <<
            p.first.j << "," << p.first.k << ")=" <<
            p.second << std::endl;
        return out;
    }
```

```cpp
private:
 struct Point
 {
     T1 i; T2 j; T3 k;
     Point(T1 p, T2 q, T3 r) : i(p), j(q), k(r) {};

     bool operator == (const Point & right) const
     {
         return (i == right.i) & (j == right.j) &
         (k == right.k);
     }
 };

 struct hashPoint
 {
     size_t operator() (const Point & p) const
     {
         return std::hash<T1>()(p.i) ^
                std::hash<T2>()(p.j) ^
                std::hash<T3>()(p.k);
     }
 };

 std::unordered_map<Point, V, hashPoint> _M;
 };
```

ABOUT THE AUTHOR

An experienced data mining engineer, passionate about technology and innovation in consumers' space. Interested in search and machine learning on massive dataset with a particular focus on query analysis, suggestions, entities, personalization, freshness and universal ranking. Antonio Gullì has worked in small startups, medium (Ask.com, Tiscali) and large corporations (Microsoft, RELX). His carrier path is about mixing industry with academic experience.

Antonio holds a Master Degree in Computer Science and a Master Degree in Engineering, and a Ph.D. in Computer Science. He founded two startups, one of them was one of the earliest search engine in Europe back in 1998. He filed more than 20 patents in search, machine learning and distributed system. Antonio wrote several books on algorithms and currently he serves as (Senior) Program Committee member in many international conferences. Antonio teaches also computer science and video game programming to hundreds of youngsters on a voluntary basis.

"Nowadays, you must have a great combination of research skills and a just-get-it-done attitude."

www.ingramcontent.com/pod-product-compliance
Lightning Source LLC
Chambersburg PA
CBHW041145050326
40689CB00001B/487